DR. TANISHA M. RANGER

Nontoxic Positivity

How to Combat the Tyranny of Positive Thinking and Craft a Genuinely Authentic Life

First edition

This book was professionally typeset on Reedsy.
Find out more at reedsy.com

To live a full and connected life in the face of difficulty and even tragedy requires the capacity to feel and make use of our emotional experience.

DIANA FOSHA
THE TRANSFORMING POWER OF AFFECT

Contents

Introduction

Welcome!

If you've purchased this book, I suspect you're a bit frustrated. I want you to know that you are not alone. We are living through a time of unprecedented struggle and collective, worldwide strife. And on so many different levels! But at the same time that we're all collectively going through this difficult time, our inability to be present with unpleasant or painful emotions is on full display.

I believe that inability to manage emotions (our own and those of others) has led to an intensification of "stay positive" culture. I, for one, am sick of it and that is why this little book exists!

I suppose I should introduce myself! My name is Tanisha. I'm a licensed psychologist practicing in Las Vegas, NV, and let me tell you these past couple of years have illuminated a lot for me about what it truly means to stay positive. I work mainly with adults who struggle with addictions, trauma, and mood disorders like depression and anxiety. It is because of my work that I've seen some of the fallout of our current cultural obsession with always appearing to be happy. Spoiler alert: it's not great!

So, I want to present you with some explanations and, more importantly, some tools that will help you to accept and address reality so that you can have joy without having to live in denial or become lost in the emptiness of false positivity. My first goal is to help you recognize and avoid the toxicity. But my BIG goal is to help you find ways to thrive despite the struggle!

Good Vibes Only

I always like to start with definitions. Let's get on the same page here. When I say "toxic positivity" what exactly do I mean?

Toxic positivity occurs when people are almost forcibly encouraged to adopt a positive attitude regardless of what they might be experiencing at any given moment. It is a demand that you minimize or completely ignore your pain and suffering, suppress your unpleasant emotions, and instead present as happy and overly optimistic.

This is a dysfunctional approach to emotion management. It's a denial of reality and, frankly, what toxic positivity is asking you to do is unnatural! I don't believe in the concept of "negative emotions." I view our emotions as messengers; they let us know what matters. We feel angry when our boundaries have been violated. We feel sad when we feel we've lost something we care about. We feel fear when we believe we are in danger. And so on. Why should a person project positivity when they are feeling anger, sadness, and fear?

We all need the space to be able to feel our feelings without being told to "fake it" so that others can feel less uncomfortable. The fact of the matter is that thinking positively, by itself, does not solve problems. But imploring someone who is going through stressful and overwhelming times to just "stay positive" can actually create more problems for them. And sometimes the call is coming from inside the house!

Yes, we can also be guilty of doing this to ourselves. It can be very insidious; causing guilt, shame, and disconnection during the very times when we need connection the most. It can stress you out even more than the actual hardship you're facing, compounding the tough time you're already experiencing because now you also get the privilege of believing it's somehow your fault.

I think it's a good idea to have some examples here, so you know exactly what I'm talking about and can recognize when toxic positivity is afoot!

Toxic positivity can sound like...

"Everything happens for a reason"

"It could've been so much worse"

"You have to stay positive"

"Crying doesn't solve anything"

"Being negative isn't gonna help"

"Just try not to think about it"

"It'll all workout in the end"

"Calm down, it's gonna be fine"

"If I could get through it, so will you"

"You're so blessed, though"

"Just let it go"

"Other people have it worse"

"God/ the universe has a plan for you"

"Just stay strong"

"If anyone can handle this, it's you"

"You have so much to be grateful for"

"You woke up that and that's something to smile about"

"It is what it is"

"You worry too much"

"Failure is not an option"

"Never give up"

"Look at the silver lining"

"Cheer up"

"There's a light at the end of the tunnel"

"Just try again"

"It was probably for the best"

"Your time will come soon enough"

"It's not that big a deal"

"Maybe it just wasn't meant to be"

"You'll be fine"

"You can't put that kind of energy out there"

"Mindset is everything"

"You just have to manifest what you want"

"You have to learn to see the good"

"At least you..."

"Have you tried..."

"Lighten up"

Okay, so obviously this list could go on forever, but I'm sure you get the point. I'm guessing that you were reading through that list with a variety of thoughts and feelings. Perhaps you recognize some phrases that have been said to you (and were aggressively unhelpful at the time). Maybe you recognize some phrases that you yourself have said (both to yourself and to others). Whatever the case, it's clear that these platitudes do not help in times of struggle or crisis. There are far better ways to be supportive.

Stop Gaslighting Yourself

Definition time! What is gaslighting? Well, I'm glad you asked! Gaslighting is a form of emotional abuse in which a person's sense of reality is attacked. Put more simply, you see something or hear or otherwise experience something. You know it. But someone is completely dedicated to making you doubt your own experience! They tell you that you didn't see the thing you thought you saw or you didn't hear the thing you thought you heard. Telling you that you don't feel those feels, those aren't your thoughts, your logic is illogical!

My friend, this is crazy-making. And when you are engaged in this toxic positivity nonsense, you are doing it to yourself. You don't deserve this! It is unreasonable to ask yourself (or anyone else) to act as if nothing is wrong, when you're struggling. It's unreasonable to demand that you (or anyone else) tamp down painful or uncomfortable emotions so as to avoid upsetting others. It is unreasonable to require (of yourself or anyone else) complete invalidation of your VERY VALID emotional experiences in the face of legitimate hardship.

Unreasonable.

The Tyranny of Positive Thinking

Perhaps what I'm saying here is a bit jarring to you. Maybe I am sounding a bit alarmist? After all, what's so wrong with staying positive? Am I supposed to just constantly be wallowing in self-pity? How is THAT better?

These are valid concerns. The thing about toxic positivity, the thing that MAKES it toxic, is that it's actually not about "staying positive" at all. At its core, it's about a denial of emotions. Perhaps even a fear of emotions. When people implore you to "keep a stiff upper lip" or "look on the bright side," what they are really asking is that you do not express your sadness, your fear, your disappointment, your pain, etc. And they aren't doing that in order to help you, they're doing it to manage their own discomfort with painful emotions, both yours and their own.

This also applies when you do it to others. But I don't want you to feel too badly about this, or beat yourself up about it. It's just a sign that you are a human being! Truly, human beings are TERRIBLE about being present with other people's pain. It's a real struggle for literally all of us. Those of us who do it well, usually have had a lot of training and done a lot of our own personal work on managing big emotions.

When someone is having a painful experience, we can often feel a bit of panic, wondering what we're supposed to do! Do we try to fix it? CAN we fix it? Are we feeling inadequate because we can't fix it? Are we feeling resentful about even having to consider this? So many things can run through our heads and, frankly, it's just easier to shut that whole situation down with an unhelpful platitude about everything happening for a reason.

It negatively impacts all of us. It invalidates all emotions that don't involve smiles. It can make us feel guilty for having those kinds of emotions and burdensome for expressing them. It often leads to feeling defective or broken because we cannot just dwell in the silver lining while the cloud is clearly in torrential downpour mode. It prevents genuine human connection, and that is devastating. Human beings are pack animals and we need each other to be able to thrive. And I think the most important negative impact is the possibility of developing or exacerbating mental health problems. Not dealing with your emotions is not a viable option. They will come out in other ways, including feeling depressed and/or anxious.

So, What Do We Do?

This is not a question in search of an answer. This is a problem in search of a solution. The difference there is that there is no magic bullet (answer), but there is a set of changes you can make (solution) to improve.

Solution: Self-Compassion!!

One thing that I've learned time and time again in the work I do as a therapist, and the work I've done with myself, is this: practicing self-compassion can absolutely transform your relationships.

The process goes like this: you begin to treat yourself with more compassion and less harsh judgment → as you decrease the amount of criticism and judgment you hurl at yourself, you feel more empathy for yourself → well, this makes it far more difficult to judge and criticize others because you're feeling more empathy for them as well → the way you interact with them is different and even if they can't name it, they feel it → and now you find that the way they interact with you is different, and BOOM! You now have a relationship that feels safer, that is less intimidating, and that is far more connected than it had been before.

So, what does this have to do with toxic positivity? Well, I view toxic positivity, when hurled at the self, as a form of judgment and harsh self-criticism. You're telling yourself that whatever it is that you are feeling in response to your experiences is not correct or not good enough. When you change that, you find yourself becoming more accepting of the entire range of emotions of which you are capable. Once you can accept that in yourself, it becomes easier to accept it in others! More details on this to come in chapter 4.

Emotion Phobia?

Let me reiterate this: I don't subscribe to the notion of positive emotions and negative emotions. I think that whole concept is dangerous and unproductive. If you start categorizing your emotions as positive or negative, you will then start trying to avoid the negative ones. It's human nature to seek out pleasure and avoid pain! It's not an effective way to live. Unfortunately, our emotions are an all-or-nothing proposition. You can't pick and choose which ones you want to experience and which ones you want to push to the side. You either allow yourself to experience the full spectrum of your human emotions or you relegate yourself to numbness. Placing value judgments like good/bad, right/wrong, positive/negative on your feelings only serves to distance you from yourself.

So, here's what I mean by emotion phobia. Like a phobia of snakes or heights or spiders or elevators, an emotion phobia occurs when people develop a fear of feeling or expressing particular emotions. It's usually a result of past traumatic experiences and often results in increased anxiety when a person even gets close to the possibility of experiencing that emotion.

They may be concerned about being overwhelmed by the emotion (eg. "if I start crying I'll never stop!"). They may have had many instances in their past in which expressing particular emotions was punished. Perhaps with ridicule, abandonment (silent treatment), or outright aggression. They may have gotten very clear messages from the environment that those specific emotions are not appropriate for them to feel (eg. "boys don't cry" or "girls don't get angry").

Whatever the reason, they have become very averse to feeling, expressing, and even acknowledging some emotions. They feel threatened by deep, authentic emotional experiences, and can often associate deficiency, inadequacy, or weakness with feeling certain emotions. As a result, they may spend a lot of time trying to avoid or suppress them, or putting up a facade so that no one can see what they're truly feeling. And let me tell you, that becomes very problematic. Here's why:

1. It robs them of the experience of the depth and breadth of human emotions available to them, which impedes self-expression
2. It prevents them from being able to learn how to process these emotions so that they can manage them and learn from those experiences
3. It denies them the opportunity to truly and deeply understand themselves, which prevents them from being able to clearly communicate their needs and wants to others and actually have them met
4. It limits their capacity for the type of emotional intimacy and connection that human beings need

In short, emotion phobia leaves you feeling incredibly isolated and perhaps even feeling broken. Suppressing your emotions can lead to symptoms of depression and anxiety. You may develop physical symptoms. And it can wreak havoc on your relationships.

Are you emotion phobic?

I think it's helpful to talk about how to recognize emotion phobia, both in yourself and in others. Mainly because understanding what's actually happening can give you the space to have more empathy for yourself and to not take things too personally when you recognize it in others.

So, here are a few things to look for:

- Do you find yourself going out of your way to avoid strong emotions in yourself or others?
- Do you minimize or even ridicule natural expressions of emotions in yourself or others?
- Do you prize being stoic in the face of emotionally charged situations, seeing that as strength?
- Do you sneer or feel disgust at even the thought expressing any level of vulnerability?

If any of those apply to you, then you may be dealing with an emotion phobia. It is worth looking into.

How can you stop being emotion phobic?

Well, dear reader, it is going to take some work! Indeed, if you are emotion phobic, it's going to require a whole paradigm shift. That is not easy. Not impossible, but definitely not easy. Certainly, the entirety of the work I do as a therapist is helping people to make the most difficult (but not impossible) changes in themselves, so as to create a life they can love!

The fact of the matter is that your phobia of particular emotions is learned. Your early environment gave you messages that dictated how you were to interact with the world, but these are not inborn traits that you carry. That is incredibly good news! You were able to learn this dysfunctional relationship with your own feelings, so that means you can learn to relate to them differently and more healthily!

The concept of emotion phobia (also called affect phobia) was developed by therapist and researcher, Dr. Leigh McCollough and before she passed away, she and her colleagues (including Dr. Kristin Osborn) used information derived from their extensive research to develop an entire model of treatment called Affect Phobia Therapy (APT). This therapy uses the same concepts that are used to treat behavioral (or external) phobias. A treatment technique called Exposure with Response Prevention and Systematic Desensitization.

Okay, I got a little jargony there!! Let me explain. When you are getting treatment for, say, a fear of heights, you will likely go through this sort of treatment. You will talk about your fear of heights and what feelings arise for you. You'll likely rate your level of distress while talking about it and your therapist will help you prevent yourself from responding in your normal way (perhaps you would change the subject and stop discussing it if you feel yourself getting worked up). Instead of that response you will practice techniques to soothe yourself. You'll do that until you can talk about it without having that emotional turmoil arise. Then you move on to what's called imaginal exposure, where you are now not just talking about the roof of the super tall building, but you are being guided by your therapist to really immerse yourself in the imagery in your mind. And then you will again practice your self-soothing techniques until imagining yourself on top of that building doesn't rile you up anymore. Then you move on to the next step and do the same things. First a relatively shorter height, then a bit higher, then higher than that.

When working in therapy to treat emotion phobia, you will essentially be doing the same thing. Identifying which emotions are problematic for you, exploring when in your history this developed, figuring out what your particular defense mechanisms look like (meaning what behaviors you engage in while trying to avoid those particular feelings), and then start the process of decreasing the heat around experiencing those emotions. The treatment is incredibly empowering because the knowledge of yourself that you develop will be unmatched! You'll be able to recognize what's happening and choose to do things differently than you had been.

But outside of therapy there are some things you can do to start to work on this.

- Make it a point to try to be present with your emotional states at any given time.
- Recognize emotions as neutral messengers helping you to

understand your experiences. They are neither negative nor positive.

- Develop your emotional literacy by working on identifying and naming what you're feeling.
- Accept that your emotions are transient, they come and go but only if you allow yourself to actually feel them.
- Understand that emotions can offer motivation and clarity when you let them.
- Recognize that your emotions are not a threat to your happiness or success.
- Remind yourself that emotions are the very foundation of relationships and you cannot have healthy ones without them.

I will say, however, that true emotion/affect phobia is usually the result of some painful childhood experiences and the best and safest way to really address this issue is in therapy.

Now, how does all this relate to toxic positivity? Well, people who struggle to experience their own emotions are usually unable to connect with themselves and other people. Toxic positivity is often used to shut down emotional expression in order to preserve comfort. Whether you are doing it to yourself or someone else, or someone is doing it to you, what we know is that there is no real empathy being expressed. Because emotional connection is required in order to feel and express empathy with others.

Simply stated, empathy is about feeling with someone. It requires you to be able to connect with a time in your life when you were experiencing similar emotions, and then express that to the other person who is suffering. You cannot offer empathy or validation if you are completely cut off from your own emotions. And truly, empathy and validation are what people (including you!) actually need when they are struggling, not empty platitudes.

How to ACTUALLY Be Positive

Okay, so we know what toxic positivity is and what makes it toxic. Now, what? Well, let's first get our definition going for healthy positivity or genuine optimism. Because, remember, positivity is not, in itself, the problem. The problem comes from using positivity as a weapon to silence and suppress experience and expression of uncomfortable emotions.

Toxic positivity sounds like: no matter what hardship or difficulty I experience I will remain positive and never let anyone see how hard this is for me.

Healthy positivity sounds like: no matter what hardship or difficulty I experience, I will remain positive in my belief that I will get through it, that it will not last forever, and that I can feel, face, manage, and express any and all emotions that arise as a result of what I'm experiencing.

I hope you can actually feel the difference in those two statements. Healthy positivity does not require you to look, act, or in any way present as if you are not suffering. It also doesn't encourage you to wallow in self-pity. Where the positivity comes in is in truly believing that you will get through it without having to minimize the "it" in order to do so.

Here is where we come back to self-compassion. What?! A SECOND definition in one chapter?! That's crazy! Well, stop clutching your pearls and listen up! I like Dr. Kristin Neff's definition and find it the most helpful. At its core, self-compassion is simply taking all of the warmth, caring, empathy, and desire to help that you readily give to others and pointing it at yourself as well. Doing this specifically and especially when you're having a difficult time, experiencing a failure, or are coming to recognize something that you don't like about yourself. Rather than meeting yourself with harsh judgment and self-criticism, you meet yourself with loving kindness and understanding.

Based on what she discovered in her research, Dr. Neff delineates three main elements of self-compassion: (1) Self-kindness, (2) Common humanity, and (3) Mindfulness.

Self-kindness: Exactly as it sounds, it's about treating yourself with kindness during your toughest moments. When you're suffering or feeling inadequate, rather than ignoring your pain and beating yourself up, you move away from self-judgment and give yourself a loving embrace. Treating yourself with the same warmth and empathy that you so willingly give to others.

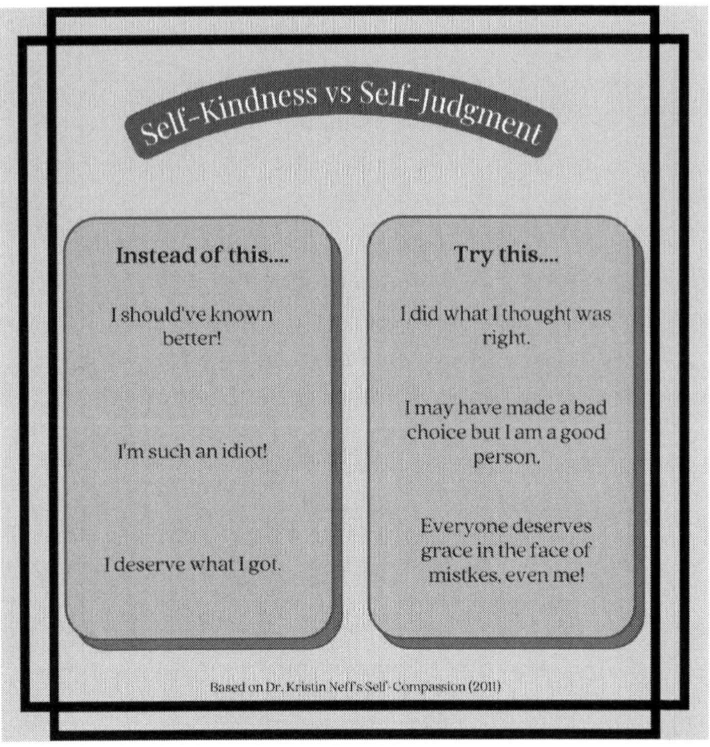

Common humanity: This one is a little less straightforward. Essentially, when we are having a difficult time, it is easy to become convinced that we are the only ones who are suffering or making these mistakes or failing in this way. It creates an intense feeling of isolation that can only be combated by embracing your common humanity. Reminding yourself that being human means being vulnerable and imperfect, and that your struggles are not a result of specific personal insufficiencies, but part of the shared human experience and something we all go through at some time or another.

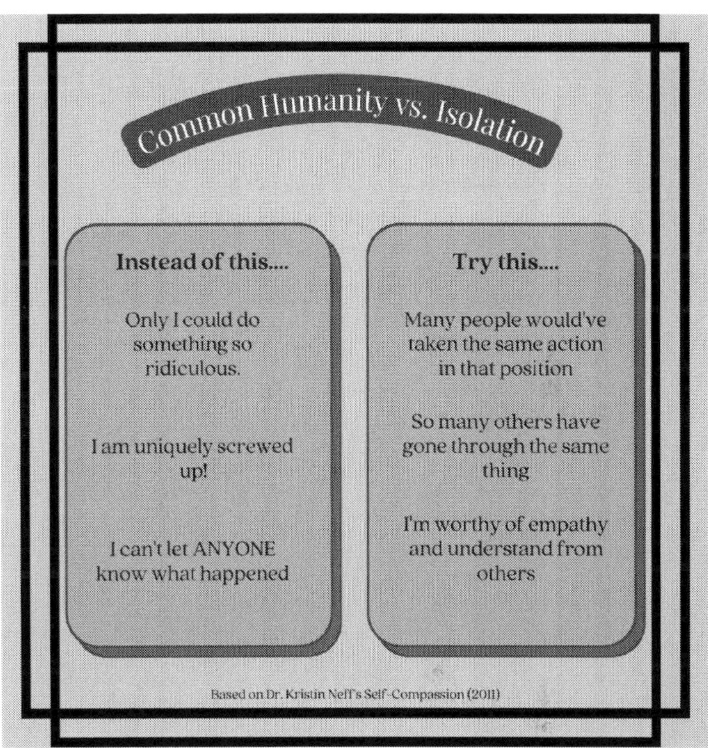

Mindfulness: I'm sure you've heard the term before, it's all over the place these days and with good reason! Mindfulness has been shown, in research studies, to be a key component in living a healthy life. A mindfulness practice can have drastic positive effects on management of so many aspects of daily life. It's no wonder everyone's talking about it! As a component of self-compassion, mindfulness serves to keep you grounded in the present. It's being able to experience your emotions without suppressing or exaggerating them. Because mindfulness is an open and non-judgmental state of being, it allows you to approach your own pain with the compassion you deserve. You cannot do that if you are ignoring your suffering.

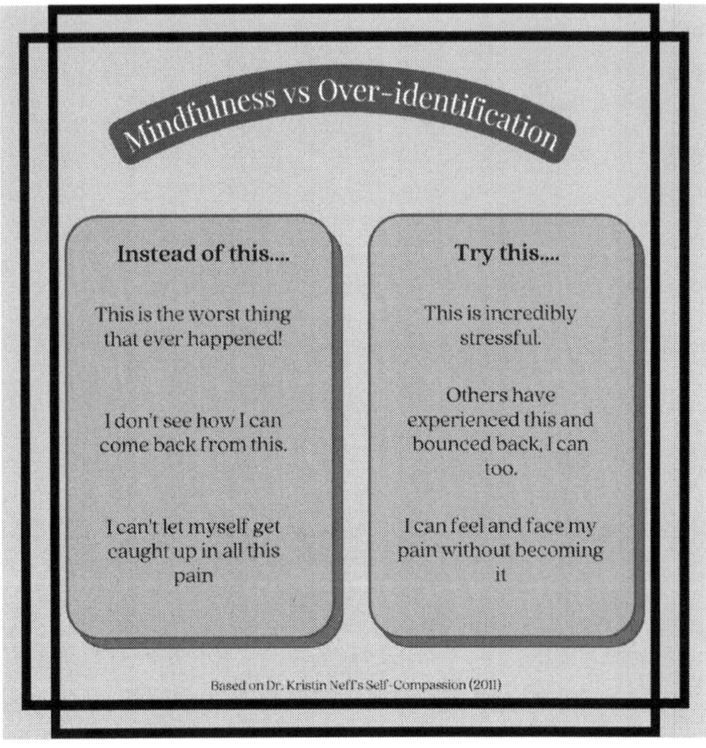

Practicing self-compassion is key when it comes to being authentically positive. When you put this into practice you will find yourself feeling less inclined to back away from your own painful emotions. You'll embrace them as a part of life and not a sign of weakness to be treated with contempt. And when you are able to do that for yourself, your capacity to do it with others grows exponentially! You won't play the toxic positivity game and you won't engage when others play it with you.

Helpful Journal Prompts

Just in case this is your first time hearing about the concept of journal prompts, let me explain. So, in my travels as a therapist I cannot count the number of times that I have encouraged my clients to take time to write in a journal. I suggest an actual notebook and actual writing utensil (as opposed to doing it digitally) because there's a level of connection to what you write that can be lost when mediated by technology. I will say, though, that I would prefer that you journal in whatever way will allow you to do so comfortably and consistently... so tech is not out of the question. Just not preferable.

What I know about the people whom I've asked to journal, is that the assignment can be incredibly anxiety provoking for most of them. Imagine, someone says something aggressively vague to you like, "I want you to keep a daily journal," with zero guidance! I would find that very upsetting... sitting and staring at a blank page. *shiver* So, I make it a point never to do that to any of my clients and I don't intend to do it to you! I'm going to offer a few journal prompts in the following categories, just to get things going for you. Categories are: Gratitude, Processing negative experiences, Self-knowledge, and Self-compassion.

The goal is to get in touch with yourself, practice being aware of your emotions without feeling overwhelmed by them, and have an historical record of your progress towards developing healthy positivity and genuine optimism in your life.

The following prompts are a mixture of things I've come up with over time and things that have been suggested by colleagues over time and things that I've come across on the internet over time. Where I can discern a specific source for where I got a particular prompt, I will name them and give them credit!

Prompts to promote gratitude

- What's the best thing that happened today?
- What's your favorite thing about yourself?
- Name one person you are exceedingly happy to have in your life and discuss why.
- Name something good you did for someone else this week.
- Name something you did this week that your future self will appreciate.
- Name something about your current life that you from ten years ago hoped and prayed for.
- Talk about a goal you set that you reached, and how you plan to celebrate it.

Prompts to process negative experiences

- How is this the best thing that ever happened to you? (Campbell Walker - see reading list)
- Write about the facts of the experience separate from the

meaning you have made about those facts.

- Consider the meaning you have attached to the experience and list out all the things "that says about you."
- Name five things you can do for self-care in the wake of this experience and then schedule the time to do them.
- Take some time to acknowledge and name all the emotions you are experiencing right now, without any value judgments.

Prompts to promote self-knowledge

- What is the worst thing you believe about yourself, and what evidence exists that supports and refutes that belief?
- What is the best thing you believe about yourself, and what evidence exists that supports and refutes that belief?
- Name something about yourself that is true now but was not true five years ago and write about how you feel about that change.
- Write about what you want your life to be about, what do you want to be known or remembered for?
- Write about times and situations in which you feel like your most authentic self and how you can cultivate more opportunities for authenticity.
- What boundaries do you need to set in order to take better care of yourself?

Prompts to promote self-compassion

- Write about a time this week when you acted with courage

despite feeling afraid.

- List three ways that you can be more supportive of yourself.
- Write about a moment this week when you chose self-kindness over self-judgment.
- Consider a failure you've experienced and discuss what you learned from it?
- Discuss five ways that you intend to practice mindfulness this upcoming week.
- Consider a stressful situation you are currently managing, what advice/support would you give a good friend who was experiencing the same concerns?
- List some regrets you have and begin the process of forgiving your past self for the choices you made when you had less information than you have now.

These are not intended to be the ONLY things you journal about as you work on this. Rather, they are intended to help you with a jumping-off point if you need one. If you don't need one, then please go forth and do your thing!

An Ode to Humanity

We have come to the close of this little life guide that I've created and I am so appreciative of your willingness to take this ride with me! Toxic positivity is a topic that is near and dear to my heart, and I am absolutely delighted to offer a bit of enlightenment. I do hope that you've found this book helpful and I welcome any and all reviews of what you've read. This chapter is the conclusion, but it's also a statement of appreciation.

Being a human is difficult, y'all. We're at the top of the food chain and yet we have so many struggles to manage! But, like Dr. Susan David says, "discomfort is the price of admission to a meaningful life." All of our growth happens outside of our comfort zone, so the struggles are inevitable but they also have the potential to be incredibly rewarding on the other side. I cannot promise you that any of this will be easy (in fact I'm sure that it won't be) but I can absolutely promise that you are worth the trouble.

Toxic positivity is a barrier to embracing your full humanness. The thing we all need when we are at our lowest moments is to know that whatever we feel is valid, and no matter what we're going through we are valued.

You are valued.

So Many Resources!

Suggested readings (books!)

- Emotional Agility - Dr. Susan David
- Self-compassion - Dr. Kristin Neff
- Your Head is a Houseboat - Campbell Walker
- The Happiness Trap - Russ Harris
- Grieving Mindfully - Dr. Sameet Kumar
- Authentic Happiness - Dr. Martin Seligman
- Finding YOUR Person - Dr. Tanisha M. Ranger

Journaling resources

- https://www.calminggrace.com/self-compassion-journal-prompts/
- https://drjotisamra.com/blog/self-compassionate-journaling-and-journaling-prompts/
- https://www.livewellwithsharonmartin.com/the-power-of-gratitude-30-days-of-gratitude-journal-prompts/
- https://grammar.yourdictionary.com/grammar/writing/40-refreshing-gratitude-journal-prompts.html
- https://skillandcare.com/self-discovery-journal-prompts

/

- https://psychcentral.com/blog/ready-set-journal-64-journaling-prompts-for-self-discovery#the-journal-prompts

Useful Websites

- https://self-compassion.org/
- https://www.affectphobiatherapy.com/

Finding a Therapist

- https://therapyforblackgirls.com/
- https://therapyforblackmen.org/
- https://www.goodtherapy.org/
- https://www.psychologytoday.com/us
- https://nqttcn.com/en/
- https://latinxtherapy.com/

About the Author

Dr. Ranger has over twenty years of experience in the mental health field and has been a licensed psychologist for a decade. She currently owns Insight to Action, a full-service private practice serving the Las Vegas Valley Area. She has worked in a wide variety of settings including: psychiatric hospitals, community mental health centers, residential treatment facilities, outpatient clinics, the Veterans Health Administration, and in private practice. Dr. Ranger has extensive training and experience treating mood disorders, racial trauma, PTSD, behavioral addictions, and relationship problems. She works exclusively with adults and older adolescents, providing individual therapy, couples therapy, and group therapy.

Dr. Ranger is a staunch advocate for educating the public about mental health, mental illness, and the steps we can take to live and thrive no matter what we might be struggling to manage. She has a particular passion for helping adult children of addiction, abuse, and dysfunction to reclaim their identities and live their lives on purpose rather than on autopilot. Dr. Ranger is trained in a number of evidence-based psychotherapies and takes a very person-centered and collaborative approach to working with her clients, tailoring treatment to each individual's needs and teaming up to address concerns.

You can connect with me on:

- https://www.insighttoaction.net
- https://twitter.com/TanishaPsyD
- https://www.facebook.com/insighttoactionpsychotherapy
- https://www.instagram.com/tanishapsyd

Also by Dr. Tanisha M. Ranger

Finding YOUR Person: The Busy Black Woman's Guide to Finding the Right Therapist for You
Finding a therapist can be difficult and disappointing when you're not sure how to start. This handbook will help you navigate the process of finding the right therapist to help you create the life of your dreams!

I will help you figure out what to look for in a therapist, where to find therapists, and how to tell if you've found your match. You'll be able to move forward with confidence as you embark on this important journey!

This handbook contains a great many resources, as well as workbook pages that you can use to take notes and answer some key questions for yourself as you go about finding your person!

Made in the USA
Middletown, DE
15 June 2023

32631733R00028